Milet Publishing
Smallfields Cottage, Cox Green
Rudgwick, Horsham, West Sussex
RH12 3DE England
info@milet.com
www.milet.com
www.milet.co.uk

First English–Korean edition published by Milet Publishing in 2013

Copyright © Milet Publishing, 2013

ISBN 978 1 84059 811 7

Original Turkish text written by Erdem Seçmen
Translated to English by Alvin Parmar and adapted by Milet

Illustrated by Chris Dittopoulos
Designed by Christangelos Seferiadis

Printed and bound in Turkey by Ertem Matbaası

My Bilingual Book

# Smell

# 냄새 맡기

English–Korean

Milet

**How do you smell a garden of flowers?**

정원의 꽃들, 아니면 소나기가 온 후 맑은 공기

**Or the fresh air after rain showers?**

냄새는 어떻게 맡습니까?

**Smell is one of our senses, as you know.**

여러분도 아시다시피, 냄새 맡기는 우리 감각들

**It's the reason you have a nose!**

중의 하나입니다. 코가 있는 것은 바로 그 이유입니다!

**Like hearing, sight, taste, and touch,**

듣기, 보기, 맛보기, 만지기와 마찬가지로 냄새

**your sense of smell tells you so much.**

맡기 감각은 여러분에게 매우 많은 것을 말해 줍니다.

**It helps you decide what you like to eat,**

이는 먹고 싶은 것과 만나고 싶지 않은 동물들을

**and animals you don't want to meet!**

정하는데 도움을 줍니다!

**Your nose is your detective for finding cakes.**

여러분의 코는 케이크를 찾는 형사인데, 반드시

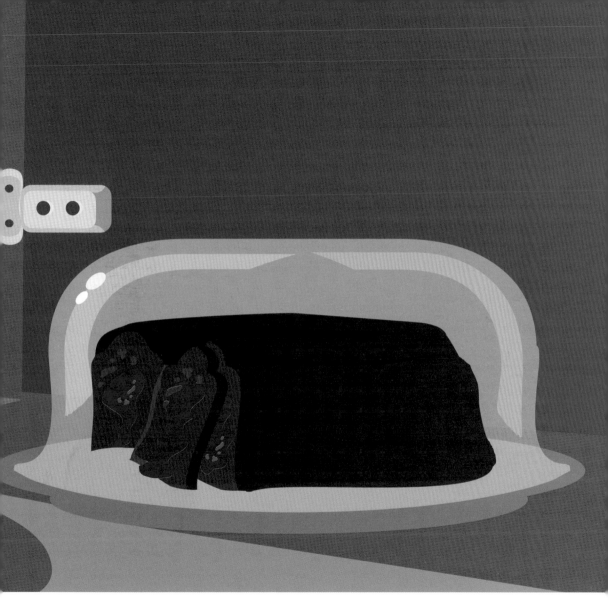

**It will track down goodies, whatever it takes!**

케이크를 찾아냅니다!

**Your smell sense tells you where you are,**

냄새 감각은 숲이나 바다 혹은 차들이 꽉 찬

**in a forest, by the sea, or in a city full of cars!**

도시에서 여러분이 어디에 있는지 말해줍니다!

**There are so many smells that we enjoy,**

비누, 빵, 가장 귀여운 장난감과 같이 우리가

**like soap and bread and our best cuddly toy!**

즐기는 매우 많은 냄새들이 있습니다!

**When you smell yourself and say, oh my gosh!**

여러분이 자신의 냄새를 맡고 "오, 맙소사!" 라고

**You know it's time for a really good wash!**

말할 때 여러분은 정말로 잘 씻어야 할 때라는 것을 압니다!

**A cold makes your nose stuffy and red,**
감기에 걸리면 코가 막히고 빨갛게 되지만

**but it will get better if you rest in bed.**

침대에서 쉬면 상태가 호전됩니다.

**And once you are well,**

그리고 일단 좋아지면, 밖으로 나가 냄새를

**go out and smell!**

맡으십시오!